OCT 1 6 2017

Cond

8m

ℓ-top

1    UT pages

# National Parks
# Great Smoky Mountains

**JOSH GREGORY**

**Children's Press®**
An Imprint of Scholastic Inc.

**Content Consultant**
James Gramann, PhD
Professor, Department of Recreation, Park and Tourism Sciences
Texas A&M University, College Station, Texas

Library of Congress Cataloging-in-Publication Data
Names: Gregory, Josh, author.
Title: Great Smoky Mountains National Park / by Josh Gregory.
Description: New York, NY : Children's Press, an imprint of Scholastic Inc., 2018. | Series: A true
  book | Includes bibliographical references and index.
Identifiers: LCCN 2016050348| ISBN 9780531233924 (library binding) | ISBN 9780531240199
  (paperback)
Subjects:  LCSH: Great Smoky Mountains National Park (N.C. and Tenn.) — Juvenile literature.
Classification: LCC F443.G7 G76 2018 | DDC 976.8/89—dc23
LC record available at https://lccn.loc.gov/2016050348

**Front cover: (main) Great Smoky
Mountains National Park at sunrise**

**Front cover (inset): A park visitor kayaking**

**Back cover: A great horned owl**

# Find the Truth!

**Everything** you are about to read is true *except* for one of the sentences on this page.

Which one is **TRUE**?

**T or F** Great Smoky Mountains National Park is the most-visited national park in the United States.

**T or F** Black bears are used to humans, so it is safe to approach them.

Find the answers in this book.

# Contents

THE **BIG** TRUTH!

## National Parks Field Guide: Great Smoky Mountains

**Great horned owl**

Tulip tree

A park visitor

There is incredible natural beauty everywhere you look in Great Smoky Mountains National Park.

# CHAPTER 1

# An Ancient Place

It has been a long day of hiking through Great Smoky Mountains National Park. Finally, you've reached the perfect spot to watch the sunset. In the valley below, a sea of green treetops stretches as far as you can see. A hazy fog hangs above the trees. The sky is colored in beautiful shades of red and orange. Hiking up here wasn't easy, but the view is more than worth the trip.

*Great Smoky Mountains National Park*

More than 100 tree species can be found in the Great Smoky Mountains.

# A Popular Park

Great Smoky Mountains National Park lies along the border between Tennessee and North Carolina. The park is part of the Great Smoky Mountains, or "Smokies," within the Appalachian Mountains. People come from all over to see the park's densely forested mountains. About 25 percent of the forestland here is **old growth**. These forests have been growing since prehistoric times without human disturbance.

# A Timeline of the Great Smoky Mountains

## 15,000 BCE
The first humans arrive in the Great Smoky Mountains region.

## 1400s CE
Cherokee and other native groups settle in the area.

## 1540
Spanish explorer Hernando de Soto is the first European to visit the Great Smoky Mountains.

# "The Place of Blue Smoke"

The Smokies were once home to the Cherokee. They called the area "the place of blue smoke." The haziness they saw in the air comes from millions of trees giving off water. The water gathers into fog.

In the late 1700s, white settlers arrived and clashed violently with the Cherokee. In the 1830s, the U.S. government forced the tribe out. Their long, difficult journey west became known as the trail of tears.

**1838–39**
The Cherokee are forced out of their homes and into Oklahoma on the Trail of Tears.

**1934**
Congress authorizes the development of Great Smoky Mountains National Park.

**1940**
President Franklin Roosevelt delivers a speech dedicating Great Smoky Mountains National Park.

# A Park's Protection

Over the course of the 1800s, more white settlers moved into the mountains and built farms. They also began chopping down trees for wood. Over time, logging became a major **industry** in the Great Smoky Mountains. Many towns were built in the region. Trees were cut down at an alarming rate. By the early 20th century, the ancient forests were in danger of disappearing completely.

To protect what was left of the forests, the U.S. government authorized the creation of Great Smoky Mountains National Park in 1934. Logging was ended, and the people living within the park's boundaries had to leave. Many of their homes and other buildings have been preserved as part of the park. As you explore, you can see these historic buildings for yourself.

# National Park Fact File

A national park is land that is protected by the federal government. It is a place of importance to the United States because of its beauty, history, or value to scientists. The U.S. Congress creates a national park by passing a law. Here are some key facts about Great Smoky Mountains National Park.

| Great Smoky Mountains National Park | |
|---|---|
| Location | Along the border between Tennessee and North Carolina |
| Year established | 1934 |
| Size | 816 square miles (2,113 sq km) |
| Average number of visitors each year | 11.3 million |
| Highest point in the park | Clingmans Dome, 6,643 feet (2,025 m) |
| Most common type of animal | Salamanders |

Many visitors use binoculars to birdwatch at Great Smoky Mountains National Park.

The Blue Ridge Parkway connects Great Smoky Mountains National Park to Shenandoah National Park in Virginia.

# CHAPTER 2

# Exploring the Park

The Great Smoky Mountains do not look like the mountains in the West. The Smokies, like the whole Appalachian range, are low and rounded. They lack the high, jagged peaks of the Rocky Mountains. These differences are because of age. At roughly 270 million years old, the Appalachians are among the planet's oldest mountains. The Rockies are much younger at 55 million to 80 million years old. The Appalachians were once just as high and harsh as the Rockies are now. Wind and water have gradually worn down the Appalachians' peaks.

# Mountains, Forests, and Streams

The Appalachian Mountains stretch almost all the way across eastern North America, running north to south. While the whole Appalachian range is low compared to the Rockies, its highest peaks lie in the Smokies. At 6,643 feet (2,025 meters), Clingmans Dome is the highest of them all. The **summit** of this mountain is home to a tower that you can climb for a view of the entire park.

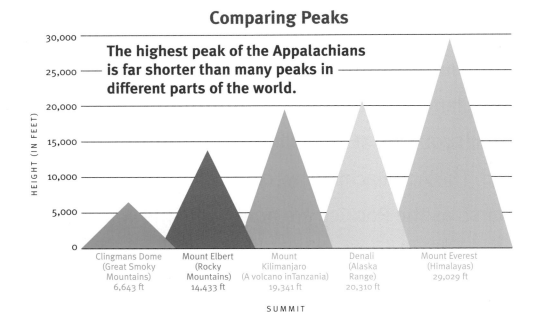

**Comparing Peaks**

The highest peak of the Appalachians is far shorter than many peaks in different parts of the world.

HEIGHT (IN FEET)

30,000
25,000
20,000
15,000
10,000
5,000
0

Clingmans Dome
(Great Smoky
Mountains)
6,643 ft

Mount Elbert
(Rocky
Mountains)
14,433 ft

Mount
Kilimanjaro
(A volcano inTanzania)
19,341 ft

Denali
(Alaska
Range)
20,310 ft

Mount Everest
(Himalayas)
29,029 ft

SUMMIT

Water spills over the rocks at Laurel Falls.

Nearly the whole park is covered in forest, from the lowest valleys to the highest peaks. There are also thousands of miles of streams flowing through the park. As they flow down to the mountains, sometimes these streams form beautiful waterfalls. Especially impressive are Laurel Falls and Abrams Falls—two of the park's most-visited places.

Cades Cove preserves historical structures from the 18th and 19th centuries.

## Plenty to Do

The Smokies are more than a collection of scenic landscapes. They are also the perfect place for outdoor activities. If you enjoy hiking, there are more than 800 miles (1,287 kilometers) of trails. These range from easy walking paths to tough wilderness adventures. If you don't want to travel on foot, you could ride a horse or a bicycle. Want to stay overnight? There are several campsites to choose from.

Fishing is another popular activity. With a state fishing license, you can cast a line in any of the park's streams during daylight hours. There are rules about how many fish you can keep, though. This helps ensure the park's fish population does not fall too low.

If you need a break from the outdoors, consider spending time at historic buildings or visitors' centers. These are great places to learn more about the park's history.

**Fly-fishing is a popular pastime at the park.**

A woodpecker carves out a nest in a tree.

# CHAPTER 3

# Amazing Animals

Although people no longer live in the area that makes up the park, plenty of animals make their home in the Smokies. There are many different **elevations** and a warm, rainy climate. These conditions allow a remarkably **diverse** range of animals to thrive. There are hundreds of species throughout the mountains, from tiny insects to enormous bears.

The park has added new names to its list of local bird species as recently as the winter of 2016-2017.

# In the Woods

About 65 **mammal** species live in the park today. It is easy to spot deer, squirrels, and chipmunks as you hike along a trail. But the park is most famous for its population of American black bears. About 1,500 of these powerful animals live in the Great Smoky Mountains. This makes the park the largest protected bear **habitat** in the eastern United States.

When deer antlers are growing, they have a soft, velvety covering.

# What to Do If You See a Bear

It is very rare for bears to attack humans. However, these huge animals can be very dangerous, especially if they have cubs to protect. If you spot a bear on your trip to the Great Smoky Mountains, do not approach it. Instead, slowly move away. Keep an eye on the bear to make sure it doesn't follow you. Don't panic if it roars or stomps its feet. Just keep moving steadily away.

**Never approach or try to feed bears!**

# From the Water to the Sky

The park's streams are home to about 67 species of fish. These include several varieties of colorful trout and chubs, as well as bass, lampreys, and many others.

If you look to the skies, you might spot any one of more than 200 bird species. Eagles, hawks, and owls soar overhead. You may see ducks, geese, and herons. Woodpeckers, hummingbirds, and colorful songbirds fill the trees. The variety is truly amazing.

If you're lucky, you might spot a bald eagle searching for prey when you visit the park.

Most of the park's salamanders do not have lungs. Instead, they breathe through their skin.

## The Salamander Capital of the World

Many reptiles and amphibians can be found in the Great Smoky Mountains. Snakes, turtles, and frogs are just a few examples. The park is famous for its enormous number of salamanders. At least 30 species of these slippery amphibians can be found there. You might spot them hanging around streams or other areas where there is plenty of moisture.

# National Parks Field Guide: Great Smoky Mountains

## Synchronous firefly

**Scientific name:** *Photinus carolinus*

**Habitat:** Most common in the Elkmont area in the north-central region of the park

**Diet:** Larvae eat snails and small insects. Adults do not eat at all.

**Fact:** Large groups of synchronous fireflies can flash their lights on and off at the same time. You can see this amazing display on special tours in the park in May and June of each year.

## Brook trout

**Scientific name:** *Salvelinus fontinalis*

**Habitat:** Large streams above 3,000 feet (914 m) in elevation

**Diet:** Insects, worms, frogs, smaller fish, and other small animals

**Fact:** The brook trout is the only trout species native to the Great Smoky Mountains.

## White-tailed deer

**Scientific name:** *Odocoileus virginianus*

**Habitat:** Found throughout the park, but most common in Cades Cove and other areas with open fields

**Diet:** Acorns, nuts, leaves, grass, and other plant foods

**Fact:** White-tailed deer are named for the bright white undersides of their tails, which they display when they are alarmed.

## Great horned owl

**Scientific name:** *Bubo virginianus*

**Habitat:** Tall trees near open areas where it can search for prey

**Diet:** Small mammals, such as mice, and birds

**Fact:** A great horned owl can kill and carry prey that is several times its own weight.

## Little brown bat

**Scientific name:** *Myotis lucifugus*

**Habitat:** Caves

**Diet:** Insects

**Fact:** A bat can eat up to 50 percent of its own weight in insects each night.

## Timber rattlesnake

**Scientific name:** *Crotalus horridus*

**Habitat:** Throughout the park's forests

**Diet:** Small mammals, birds, amphibians, and other snakes

**Fact:** The timber rattlesnake is one of only two **venomous** snake species in the park.

# The Colors of Nature

Because the Great Smoky Mountains are covered in thick forests, it is no surprise they are home to an amazing range of plant life. Thousands of different plants can be seen along the park's trails. There are enormous trees and colorful wildflowers. As you walk, you'll brush up against grasses, ferns, and shrubs.

You can use webcams online to check the current air quality in Great Smoky Mountains National Park.

Tulip trees get their name from the shape of their flowers.

## Trees Everywhere

Trees drew settlers to the Great Smoky Mountains long ago. They remain one of the area's greatest attractions today. Mountain peaks are covered in beautiful evergreen trees such as spruces and firs. At lower elevations, you'll find cherry trees, walnut trees, and many other **deciduous** trees. Most amazing are the park's enormous tulip trees. Their blooms are shaped like tulip flowers and their trunks can grow up to 7 feet (2 m) across.

# Autumn Leaves

Each fall, the stunning foliage of the Great Smoky Mountains draws huge crowds to the park. The leaves on trees at higher elevations, where the temperatures are cooler, start changing in mid-September. As the season goes on, the fall colors spread down the mountains. The leaves turn vibrant shades of yellow, orange, red, and purple. Driving or hiking through the park at this time of year is an unforgettable experience.

Leaves turn an incredible variety of colors during the fall in the Great Smoky Mountains.

# Wondrous Wildflowers

Fall isn't the only time you can see gorgeous color in the Great Smoky Mountains. The park is also famous for its astonishing range of wildflowers. There are more than 1,500 kinds of flowering plants growing within its boundaries. That is more than in any other U.S. national park. Different kinds bloom at different times of year, so you can enjoy a colorful view no matter when you visit.

**The flowers of the Smokies come in all sizes, shapes, and colors.**

The fringed phacelia is just one of the many ephemeral flower species at the park.

Some of the most impressive flowers in the park belong to a group called ephemerals. "Ephemeral" means passing quickly, and these flowers do just that. They grow up from underground, bloom, and wither away all within a few weeks each year. You can only catch a glimpse of these beautiful, short-lived flowers if you visit the park during the spring.

# CHAPTER 5

# Protecting the Park

Like all outdoor environments, the Great Smoky Mountains rely on a delicate natural balance to stay healthy. When this balance is thrown off, it can lead to big problems for the park's air, water, soil, and wildlife. To protect against environmental damage, experts monitor the park closely. They also come up with creative plans for dealing with potential problems.

 The park receives about 60,000 visitors per day on summer weekends.

# Problems With Pollution

One major problem in the park is a decline in air quality. Cars, factories, and power plants in the area all release dangerous chemicals into the air. Wind blows this polluted air into the park. There, it reduces how far people can see from scenic viewpoints. It also damages plants, water, and soil. This leads to problems for the wildlife that rely on those things to survive. To fight these issues, the National Park Service works closely with lawmakers to create regulations designed to help keep pollution in check.

**Studies show that the air quality in the park is similar to that of Los Angeles, one of the nation's largest cities.**

Fires might seem like a disaster, but they are essential for the park's health.

# Fire in the Park

Wildfires happen naturally in the Great Smoky Mountains, usually about twice a year. The park used to put all these fires out. However, experts learned that wildfires add nutrients to the soil and help plants grow. Fires also clear out dense areas to make space for animals. Today, park officials let most wildfires burn, unless they threaten lives or homes. Officials even start some controlled fires purposely to reduce dead plant material.

red marking

Red-cockaded woodpeckers are among the many endangered species to make the park home.

# Wildlife in Danger

Intentional fires are one tool the park service uses to help support species that are in trouble of disappearing. There are many threatened and **endangered** plant and animal species in the park. Keeping these species safe from extinction is a priority for the park service. One way it accomplishes this is by making sure that rare species have plenty of safe spaces to breed and raise young. Controlled fires help create places for the endangered red-cockaded woodpecker to build nests.

# Unwanted Invaders

**Invasive** species can be a major threat to native wildlife. In the Smokies, invasive woolly adelgids threaten one of the park's most common trees, the eastern hemlock. The adelgids are Asian insects that reached the Great Smoky Mountains in about 2002. Adelgids feed on hemlock trees, often killing them in the process. To fight these insects, the park is using special chemicals. It has also introduced beetles to feed on the adelgids.

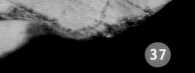

# Bringing Species Back

Some species that once lived in the Great Smoky Mountains were wiped out within the region long ago. For example, overhunting killed off the area's elk population well before the park was founded. Today, experts are working to bring long-gone species back to the park. Elk were reintroduced starting in 2001. Peregrine falcons, river otters, and several types of fish have also been brought back to the area.

If you see an elk, enjoy it from a distance. Park rules prohibit visitors from approaching elk.

Volunteers collect litter along one of the park's roads.

# Helping Out

Anyone can help protect the Great Smoky Mountains. If you visit, follow the rules. Don't litter, damage plants, or bother animals. "Take only pictures, leave only footprints," is a good rule when visiting any protected environment. You can help at home, too. Use less electricity to help reduce air pollution. Even if you live far from the park, cleaner air everywhere is good for all our natural resources. By thinking of the environment in our everyday lives, we can help preserve our parks for years to come. ★

# Map Mystery

Many historic buildings have been preserved in one particular area of Great Smoky Mountains National Park. What is it called? Follow the directions to find the answer.

**Compass Rose**

North
West — East
South

Laurel Creek Road

Cades Cove

**Cades Cove Visitor Center**

Appalachian Trail

Tennessee
North Carolina

Fontana L

Nantahala National Forest

## Directions

1. Start at the Sugarlands Visitor Center.

2. Go southwest to the Elkmont Campground.

3. Continue west to the Great Smoky Mountains Institute.

4. Travel northwest to Laurel Creek Road.

5. Follow the road south and west to reach your destination.

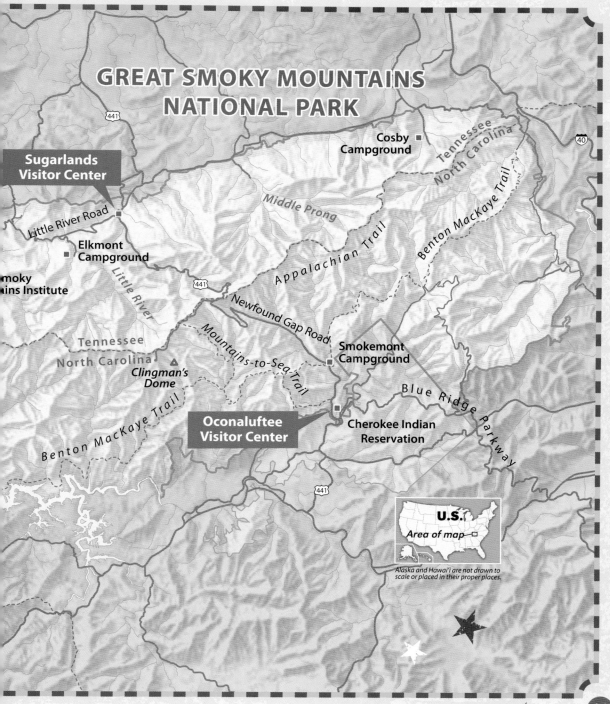

# GREAT SMOKY MOUNTAINS NATIONAL PARK

Cosby Campground

Tennessee
North Carolina

Benton MacKaye Trail

Sugarlands Visitor Center

Middle Prong

Little River Road

Appalachian Trail

Elkmont Campground

Little River

moky
ins Institute

Newfound Gap Road

Mountains-to-Sea Trail

Smokemont Campground

Tennessee
North Carolina

Clingman's Dome

Benton MacKaye Trail

Oconaluftee Visitor Center

Cherokee Indian Reservation

Blue Ridge Parkway

**U.S.**

*Area of map*

*Alaska and Hawai'i are not drawn to scale or placed in their proper places.*

**Answer:** Cades Cove

# Be an ★ ★ Animal Tracker!

If you're ever in Great Smoky Mountains National Park, keep an eye out for these animal tracks. They'll help you know which animals are in the area.

### Elk
**Hoof length:** 3 inches (8 cm)

### White-tailed deer
**Hoof length:** 4 inches (10 cm)

## Black bear

**Paw length:** 4.5 inches (11 cm)

## Great horned owl

**Foot length:** 3 inches (8 cm)

## White-footed mouse

**Paw length:** 0.25 inches (0.6 cm)

## Gray squirrel

**Paw length:** 2 inches (5 cm)

**Percent of the park that is forested:** 95

**Percent of the forests that are old growth:** 25

**Total length of streams in the park:** About 2,030 mi. (3,267 km)

**Total length of trails in the park:** More than 800 mi. (1,287 km)

**Number of mammal species in the park:** About 65

**Number of bird species:** More than 200

**Number of reptile and amphibian species:** More than 80, including at least 30 types of salamander

**Number of native trout species:** 1

## Did you find the truth?

**T** Great Smoky Mountains National Park is the most-visited national park in the United States.

**F** Black bears are used to humans, so it is safe to approach them.

# Resources

## Books

Flynn, Sarah Wassner, and Julie Beer. *National Parks Guide U.S.A.* Washington, DC: National Geographic, 2016.

McMahan, F. Carroll. *Sevierville*. Charleston, SC: Arcadia Publishing, 2012.

Tornio, Stacy, and Ken Keffer. *Ranger Rick: National Parks!* Lanham, MD: Muddy Boots, 2016.

**Visit this Scholastic website for more information on Great Smoky Mountains National Park:**
★ www.factsfornow.scholastic.com
Enter the keywords **Great Smoky Mountains**

# Important Words

**deciduous** (di-SIJ-oo-uhs) shedding all leaves every year in the fall

**diverse** (di-VURS) having many different types or kinds

**elevations** (el-uh-VAY-shuhnz) heights above sea level

**endangered** (en-DAYN-jurd) at risk of becoming extinct, usually because of human activity

**habitat** (HAB-i-tat) the place where an animal or plant is usually found

**industry** (IN-duh-stree) a type of business or trade

**invasive** (in-VAY-sihv) describing a plant or animal that is introduced into a new habitat and may cause it harm

**mammal** (MAM-uhl) a warm-blooded animal that has hair or fur and usually gives birth to live babies

**old growth** (OLD GROHTH) describing forests that have developed over a long period of time without major human or natural changes

**summit** (SUHM-it) the highest point

**venomous** (VEN-uhm-uhs) able to produce poison and pass it into a victim's body through a bite or sting

# Index

Page numbers in **bold** indicate illustrations.

# About the Author

Josh Gregory is the author of more than 100 books for kids. He has written about everything from animals to technology to history. A graduate of the University of Missouri-Columbia, he currently lives in Portland, Oregon.